THE
COINS AND TOKENS

OF

NOVA SCOTIA

BY

EUGENE G. COURTEAU, M. D.

Sanford J. Durst
Numismatic Publications
New York, N.Y.

TABLE OF CONTENTS

Copyright
©
1982

Sanford J. Durst
170 East 61st Street
New York, NY 10021

ISBN No.   0-942666-09-7
L.C. No.   82-70839

Originally Published
By the Author
St. Jacques, Quebec, Canada
1911

This is a reprint

INTRODUCTION

Twelve years ago when I began to collect in a systematic manner, I wondered why Canadian numismatic writers gave so many details in describing the different varieties of some issues (which I approve) while totally neglecting others, despite their great historical importance and comparative rarity.

For instance the tokens which make the subject of this work are full of interest; those issued by the merchants give an idea of the extension of trade in Nova Scotia at that period, the Broke issues which reminds one of the famous events of the war of 1812 and commemorates the valor of the gallant Commander, and last but not the least, the thistle series which recalls to the inhabitants of Scotch descent the emblem of their motherland.

So with the hope of helping Collectors interested in Canadian tokens I undertake the task of describing all varieties of the coins and tokens of Nova Scotia that have come under my notice with their degrees of rarity.

I have purposely omitted the description of specimens known as pattern pieces.

Before closing let me request the young students not to be too critical of this effort, especially as to the degrees of rarity which in this series is very difficult to accurately adjust. This because several are here described for the first time from specimens in my collection which are the only ones known to me.

It should be understood that specimens rated R. 1 are easily obtainable, whereas those rated R. 7 or 8 are very rare, R. 9 of the utmost rarity and R. 10 unique.

When no mention is made of the metal or of the kind of edge in describing the tokens, it should be understood that in the one case the metal is copper and in the other that the edge is the same as that of the preceding number.

EUGENE G. COURTEAU,
St-Jacques, Que.,
Canada.

1st June, 1910.

BIBLIOGRAPHY AND SUGGESTED READING:

Breton, P.N., **ILLUSTRATED HISTORY OF COINS & TOKENS RELATING TO CANADA**

Charlton, J.E., **STANDARD CATALOG OF CANADIAN COINS**

Charlton, J.E. and Willey, R.C., **STANDARD GRADING GUIDE TO CANADIAN DECIMAL COINS**

Courteau, E., **THE COPPER TOKENS OF THE BANK OF MONTREAL**

Courteau, E., **THE WELLINGTON TOKENS RELATING TO CANADA**

Haxby, J.A. and Willey, R.D., **COINS OF CANADA**

Koper, B., **CANADIAN PROVINCIAL COPPER CENTS**

Le Roux, J., **THE CANADIAN COIN CABINET**

McLachlan, R.W., **THE COPPER TOKENS OF UPPER CANADA**

Wood, H., **THE CANADIAN BLACKSMITH COPPERS**

PROVINCE OF NOVA SCOTIA

Thistle Series.

1823 Half-pennies.

No. 251.

Obv. Bust of George IV to the left, laureated. PROVINCE OF NOVA SCOTIA. The laurel wreath shows 15 leaves; the upper lock of hair on forehead is the longest and points to letter o; the drapery is fastened on shoulder by a small, circular rosette.

Rev. A thistle sprig. HALFPENNY TOKEN 1823. The left thistle leaf has 20 notches, and the stem points directly to the center of 8 in the date. Engrailed edge. R. 1.

15 *leaves.*

No. 252.

Obv. Laurel wreath has 14 leaves; the longest lock on forehead extends between the letters o and F.

Rev. The left leaf has 22 notches, the stem is straight and almost touches figure 8, to the right. R. 1.

14 *leaves.*

No. 253.

Obv. The wreath has 13 leaves; the shape of the 3 locks on forehead is peculiar to this variety, the middle one being much the largest and curving downward; the ribbon is weakly struck—left end barely shows, and the bust comes down lower than letter P.

Rev. Left leaf has 21 notches; the stem points to the center of 8. R. 4.

13 *leaves.*

No. 254.

Obv. There are only 2 locks of hair on forehead, both pointing upward. The distinguishing feature of this variety is in the absence of hyphen between NOVA and SCOTIA.

Rev. Closely resembles No. 252, the left leaf has as many notches, but terminates in line with the thistle head and its points are differently arranged; the stem comes down close to the top of 8, to the right. R. 5.

13 *leaves.*

No. 255.

Obv. Same as No. 254.

Rev. Left leaf has 20 notches; the stem is much curved and its end touches the top of figure 8, to the right. R. 7.

13 *leaves.*

No. 256.

Obv. Laurel wreath has 12 leaves with only one at top, longer than hair—the only instance; there are 2 small locks of hair under 3 large ones of uniform size on forehead.

Rev. Same as No. 253. R. 7.

12 *leaves.*

No. 257.

Obv. Laurel wreath has also 12 leaves, but the 5 locks on forehead are smaller and of equal size; there are 2 long locks of hair extending close to letter N. Prominent neck.

Rev. Left leaf has 19 notches, stem touches figure 8, to the right. R. 8.

12 *leaves.*

1824. Half pennies.

No. 258.

Obv. Similar. Laurel wreath has 4 leaves at top, P away from bust; star-shaped button fastening drapery.

Rev. Similar, but date 1824. Left leaf extends above thistle head, figures in date widely spaced. R. 4.

4 *top-leaves.*

No. 259.

Obv. The wreath has 3 leaves at top and the bust is close to P.
Rev. Left leaf ends in line with thistle head, figures in date closer together.   R.   3.
3 *top-leaves.*

1824.   Pennies.

No. 260.

Obv. Similar.   Laurel wreath has 4 leaves at top, the second touches foot of letter F, to the right; the ends of the ribbon which tie the wreath are straight and forked; the drapery is fastened by a star-shaped button.
Rev. ONE PENNY TOKEN 1824.   The thistle stem though closer to 8 than to 2 points towards the latter.   R.   7.
4 *top-leaves.*

No. 261.

Obv. The 3 leaves at top are distant from F; the middle lock of a group of three behind top-leaves is the longest and extends to the foot of N, the left is thin and distant from same letter; the ribbon-ends are plain and drapery fastened by a circular button.
Rev. Resembles No. 260, but the longest inside point of left leaf is closer to the bulb, and the letter K is double-cut.   R.   2.
3 *top-leaves.*

No. 262.

Obv. Closely resembles No. 261, but the 3 locks behind the leaves are thick, of equal height and close to N, and the small locks of hair on neck terminate in a straight way.   All the specimens I have seen so far present this peculiarity, the upper horizontal line of letter E does not extend beyond the perpendicular.

This obverse seems to be from a retouched die of the preceding number.
Rev. Same as No. 261.   R.   5.
3 *top-leaves.*

No. 263.

Obv. The first of the 3 leaves at top touches F; the ribbon-ends are curved downward and forked; drapery fastened by a star-shaped button. In SCOTIA, the letter A is entirely under the bust—the only case in which this occurs.

Rev. Thistle stem long, midway from 8 and 2, but pointing towards the latter figure. R. 3.

3 *top-leaves.*

No. 264.

Obv. Same as No. 263.
Rev. Same as No. 261. R. 6.
3 *top-leaves.*

1832. Half=pennies.

An easy way to classify the regular half-pennies under their proper numbers is to divide them into three groups: the first, on which the left end of the ribbon which ties the wreath is the longer, No. 265 (illustrated); the second, on which the right ribbon is the longer, Nos. 266, 267, 268, 269, 270 and 271; and the third group, where both ends of the ribbon are equal, Nos. 272, 272a, 273, 274, 275 and 276.

Once divided into groups, Collectors should note the relative position and the difference in size and shape of the three locks of hair standing on forehead, also note whether the central leaf of a group of three near bow overlaps adjacent ones, or is partially covered by them.

The points of difference between each variety are so minute that I thought best to illustrate but one, No. 265.

It is to be noted that the 1832 half-pennies and pennies bear the same portrait as to that of the 1823 and 1824 tokens, although William IV had been reigning for two years.

GROUP I. Left ribbon the longer.

8

No. 265.

Obv. The 3 locks of hair on forehead are small and equally distant; the central leaf of a group of three near bow partially overlaps lower one; ribbon which ties the wreath is broader than on any other of the series, its left end is straight, touches drapery and comes down lower than the right.

Rev. A thistle sprig. HALF PENNY TOKEN 1832. The die used in the striking of the reverses of these regular half-pennies (No. 270 excepted) has been retouched at least three or four times.   R.   1.

GROUP II.   Right ribbon the longer.

No. 266.

Obv. The middle lock is the smallest and about midway from others, which are large; central leaf near bow partially overlaps adjacent ones; the right ribbon is the longer and its end turns outward.

Rev. Same as No. 265.   R.   1.

No. 267.

Obv. Locks on forehead almost straight (superposed upon each other), the upper one is the smallest; central leaf near bow slightly covered by others; right ribbon a trifle the longer.

Rev. Same as No. 265.   R.   1.

No. 268.

Obv. The lower lock is heavy and its end hook-shaped, the middle, which is the smallest, is disconnected from upper one; the upper leaf near bow is clearly distinct from central one and separated from knot; right ribbon the longer.

Rev. Same as No. 265.   R.   3.

No. 269.

Obv. The locks on forehead are small, disconnected and of equal size, a single hair runs from lower lock to the left (a peculiarity found only on this variety); the central leaf near bow is partially covered by adjacent ones, right ribbon the longer.

Rev. Same as No. 265, but from two states of the die; one is from a slightly broken and worn die.   R.   4.

9

No. 270.

Obv. Locks on forehead equally distant, the two upper ones are long and very thin, and end in small downward curves; central leaf near bow slightly overlaps others; right ribbon narrow and the longer.

Rev. Closely resembles No. 265, but the notches around the leaves are not so widely cut, and the figures in the date are lighter. R. 4.

No. 271.

Obv. The two lowest locks are small and close together, the upper one is a trifle larger and blunt instead of being pointed as all the others are. The upper part of the nose, the bow and the ribbon are weakly struck, hence bow disconnected from knot and left ribbon detached; right ribbon the longer.

Rev. Same as No. 265, but after the die had been retouched, probably for the fourth time. R. 6.

GROUP III. Ribbons of equal length.

No. 272.

Obv. The two upper locks are thin, disconnected and almost straight, the middle is closer to lower one; the leaves near bow show all, but the upper one is disconnected from knot; the ribbons are much in relief, are close to the neck and of equal length, the left terminates in an outward curve.

Rev. Same as No. 265, but die slightly touched up. R. 2.

No. 272a.

Obv. The two lowest locks are long, the middle is longer on this than on any other of the series, and comes very close to letter o, the upper one is thick and short; the leaves near bow show all, and the upper one is well connected to knot; ribbons of equal length.

Rev. Same as No. 265, but from a slightly retouched die. R. 6.

I am indebted to Mr. Ludger Gravel, of Montreal, for this variety, which he had the kindness to give me. I found it in his collection at the very last moment.

No. 273.

Obv. The two upper locks are short and thick, and distant from lower one; the central leaf near bow is partially hidden by adjacent ones; both ends of the ribbon are straight and equal.

Rev. Same as No. 265, but from first state of die. There is also what one may call a second reverse from same die after it had been slightly repaired; especially so at the right leaf, where a point of a group of two, opposite N in TOKEN, is plain and heavy instead of being divided, as it is on all the other varieties. Those from the first state of the die are somewhat scarcer, and I style them the "small thistle" varieties. R. 1.

No. 274.

Obv. The two upper locks are plain, the middle is the smallest, almost straight, and is closer to lower one; the leaves near bow are all visible and well connected to the knot; narrow ribbons of equal length. A single hair forming an upward curve under the lower lock is peculiar to this variety.

Rev. Same as No. 265. R. 1.

No. 275.

Obv. The locks on forehead are equally distant and the middle one forked; central leaf partially overlaps others; the ribbons are the same length, but the left is detached and terminates in an outward curve.

Rev. Same as No. 265, but from first state of die. R. 2.

No. 276.

Obv. The two lowest locks are large, the upper one is small and weakly struck, almost imperceptible; the three leaves near bow entirely show and are well connected to knot; the ribbons are of equal length and narrower than on any other of the series.

Rev. Same as No. 271. R. 7.

No. 277.

Obv. Similar. (The so-called counterfeits.) There are also 3 locks of hair on forehead, the upper one touches F; the ribbon shows but one end which curves downward and is distant from drapery; the latter is fastened by a large, oval rosette, composed of small dots.

Rev. Left leaf has 18 notches; the stem is sharp and points to figure 3. R. 7.

18 *notches*.

No. 278.

Obv. The upper lock on forehead extends to and touches o; there are no locks of hair on neck, under leaves; the ribbons are straight and close to drapery, which is fastened by a plain, oval rosette.

Rev. Same as No. 277. R. 1.

18 *notches*.

No. 279.

Obv. Same as No. 278. Brass. R. 5.

No. 280.

Obv. Same as No. 278.

Rev. Erroneous date, 1382. Left leaf has also 18 notches but differently arranged; the thistle head is larger and closer to letter Y, the base of which is double-cut; sharp stem pointing between 3 and 8 in date, but closer to the last figure. R. 8.

18 *notches*.

I am greatly indebted to Mr. H. L. Doane, of Truro, N.S., for having lent me this variety in order to get it illustrated. If it had not been for the courtesy and kindness of this gentleman the illustration of this interesting coin would be wanting.

The error in the date, the poor and inaccurate illustrations of this token in the previous books have always led me to the belief that it was an imposition. But through the kindness of Mr. R. W. McLachlan, of Montreal, I had the opportunity to compare his specimen with that of Mr. Doane, and found them exactly the same, and that both reverses were from one and an original die.

Moreover, a careful comparison of the 1382 variety with the others shows plainly the close relationship existing between all the counterfeit half-pennies, as will be proven under their respective numbers, and still confirms me in my belief that the erroneous date is genuine.

This is how the error probably occurred, when the reverse die of No. 277 began to give way the issuers of these tokens ordered another die to be made, on which the engraver, most likely by inadvertance, transposed the figures in the date, making it read 1382.

As soon as the error was discovered, they (the issuers) got the date corrected and the die retouched twice, and kept on using it, but this time with an other obverse die—the " curved ribbon " variety.   Probably on account that the first die used—the " straight ribbon " variety—began to wear out, and also showed in incused letters the word TOKEN under SCOTIA.

This would explain the scarcity of the erroneous date, No. 280, and the blunders appearing in the dates of the subsequent varieties, namely, Nos. 281 and 282.

The issue of these counterfeit tokens was most likely ordered by Retail Merchants, probably of Montreal, and the dies made in imitation of the regular ones. Similar counterfeiting had already occurred of the 1812 Tiffin half-pennies and the 1820 Harp and Bust series.

I have found great pleasure in collecting these accidental, or error pieces, and they should prove interesting to all Canadian Collectors, as they are mementoes of the great monetary struggle our country had to sustain during the first half of the nineteenth century.

No. 281.

Obv. Same as No. 277, but from a slightly rusted and broken die.
Rev. Left leaf has 16 notches and a small shoot at the base—so have the two following varieties; the stem is sharp and points between 8 and 3, but is closer to last figure.   R. 5.
16 notches.

This reverse is from the same die as to that of the preceding number after the date had been changed to 1832 and the leaves retouched.   On good specimens a faint line, representing the top of figure 3, can be seen under the 8, and the new cut 3 has retained a little the form of an 8.   This explains that at first glance the date of this variety reads 1882.

The scarcity of the erroneous date and the comparatively high prices obtained for good specimens have induced some unscrupulous speculator to alter the date of this piece, so that it appears to be 1382.

The imposition is easily detected, the genuine 1382 is always found with the " straight ribbon " obverse, and the 3 in the date is old style, that is, it has a square top.

I have in my collection a copy of this imposition which, though poorly done, can be passed to young Collectors as genuine.

No. 282.

Obv. Same as No. 277, but from a broken die. Although the break under the nose is larger than on the preceding number, the die shows plainly that it has been repaired.

Rev. Left leaf has 15 notches; the seeds on the bulb are larger; stem broken square, and though nearer to 3 than to 8 points towards the last figure. From same die as to that of preceding number after it had been considerably retouched. R. 3.

15 *notches.*

No. 283.

Obv. Same as No. 277. This die begins to show some defects.

Rev. Closely resembles No. 282, but the left leaf has only 13 notches and the seeds on bulb are more numerous. R. 6.

13 *notches.*

Numbers 277 to 283, both inclusive, are generally known as counterfeits, so are numbers 286, 287 and 288.

1832. Pennies.

No. 284.

Obv. Similar type to No. 265. The bow is distant from the head and the ribbon from the neck, the ends of which are cut square and of equal length.

Rev. ONE PENNY TOKEN, 1832. R. 1.

No. 285.

Obv. Closely resembles No. 284, but the bow is closer to the head, the ribbon to the neck, with its left end straight and longer.

Rev. Same as No. 284. R. 2.

No. 285a.

Obv. Closely resembles the last, but the bow touches head and the ribbon is farther from the neck, its left end comes down a trifle below the right and turns slightly outward.

Rev. Same as No. 284.   R. 7.

Mr. S. S. Heal, of Toronto, was the first to call my attention to this variety, which may be considered somewhat scarce.

No. 286.

Obv. Similar.   (So-called counterfeits.)   The ribbon is of un-equal width, the bottom-end being the widest; the drapery is fastened by an oval rosette.

Rev. Light stem pointing between 8 and 3.   On this and on number 289, the figure 2 is disproportionately large.   R. 2.

No. 287.

Obv. There are 3 locks of hair on forehead, the middle one is the largest, the upper points to the leaf; the ribbons are well pro-portionate with the bow.

Rev. The stem is heavy and the figure 2 small.   Of these three counterfeit pennies, this is certainly the best executed.   R. 2.

No. 288.

Same as No. 286, but brass.   R. 5.

No. 289.

Obv. Ribbon ends blocked and resembling a beaver's tail; drapery fastened by a circular rosette.

Rev. Larger thistle with one point of left leaf extending between ONE and PENNY; the stem is above 3 and close to it.   R. 4.

No. 289a.

Same as No. 289, but brass.   R. 5.

1840.   Half-pennies.

No. 290.

Obv. Bust of Queen Victoria to the left, with hair brushed back in coil or Psyche knot. The upper lip extends diagonally in line with the tip of the nose, which gives the features a strange appearance; a pendent lock comes directly from the left of coil. In legend, the letters are perfect.

This obverse when found in combination with the large " O " reverse is from a rusted die.

Rev. HALFPENNY TOKEN 1840. The size of the figures in date gradually increases from 1 to 0, with the last figure too large.   R. 4.

Large O.

No. 291.

Obv. Perfect lip. The end of middle part of coil connects with that of lower one; the lock coming from hair coil is a trifle to the left. The inner part of each foot of letter A in SCOTIA does not come up well or is totally wanting.

Rev. Same as No. 290.   R. 6.

Large O.

No. 292.

Obv. Perfect lip. The lower part of hair coil does not extend to the body of same and is distant from middle part; the lock is small, almost touches head and comes from centre of coil. Perfect letters in legend.

Rev. In the date, the figure 4 is too large, the 0 of medium size when compared with those of the large and the small 0 varieties. R. 1.

Medium sized O.

No. 293.

Obv. Closely resembles the last, but the mouth is more open and the nose longer; the inner part of each foot of A, both in NOVA and SCOTIA, is wanting.

Rev. Same as No. 292.   R. 3.

Medium sized O.

No. 294.

Obv. Same as No. 290.
Rev. Same as No. 292.   R. 2.
Medium sized O.

No. 295.

Obv. The outline of the nose opposite the eye is wanting; upper part of coil distant from head; the lock is long, comes from the right of coil and turns downward The lip and letters are perfect.

Rev. In the date, the figure 4 is too large, the 0 small.   R. 2.

Small 0.

No. 296.

Obv. Same as No. 290.

Rev. Resembles No. 295, but the thistle head is larger, the group of points inside of the right leaf, opposite the stem, has 3 instead of 4, and the 0 in the date is nearer to 4.   R. 5.

Small 0.

No. 297.

Obv. The middle part of coil ends within the curve of lower one; the pendent lock is short and heavy, and comes directly from the centre of coil.

Rev. Same as No. 295.   R. 5.

Small 0.

No. 298.

Obv. Resembles No. 291, but the lock comes directly from the centre of coil and points downward; the letters PVE in PROVINCE are partially double-cut—the only variety presenting this peculiarity.

Rev. Same as No. 296.   R. 7.

Small 0.

1843.   Half-pennies.

No. 299.

Obv. Same as No. 291.

Rev. Similar, but dated 1843.   There are 14 seeds around the thistle bulb and 14 thorns on stem—a short one pointing upward under left leaf; the stem points between figures 8 and 4.   R. 3.

14 *thorns.*

No. 300.

Obv. Resembles No. 290, but the upper lip is still more prominent, the lock heavier and coming from the right of the coil.
Rev. Resembles No. 299, but there are only 13 seeds around the bulb, and the right leaf, inside and opposite the stem, is one notch less.   R. 5.
14 *thorns.*

No. 301.

Obv. The pendent lock is thin and comes directly from centre of coil.   In SCOTIA, the upper stroke of letter S is double-cut and the left foot of A stands higher than that of letter I.
Rev. Same as No. 300.   R. 4.
14 *thorns.*

No. 302.

Obv. Same as No. 300.
Rev. Resembles No. 299, but there are 15 seeds around the bulb and only 10 thorns on stem, with one, almost horizontal, under left leaf; the stem points towards 8.   R. 4.
10 *thorns.*

No. 303.

Obv. Same as No. 301.
Rev. Same as No. 302.   R. 1.
10 *thorns.*

No. 304.

Obv. Same as No. 301.
Rev. Resembles No. 300, but the thistle is larger, has also 13 seeds around the bulb, but only 9 thorns on stem, with none under left leaf.   R. 5.
9 *thorns.*

<h2 style="text-align:center">No. 305.</h2>

Obv. Same as No. 291.
Rev. Same as No. 304. R. 6.
9 *thorns.*

<h2 style="text-align:center">No. 306.</h2>

Obv. Same as No. 291.
Rev. Resembles No. 302, but there are only 13 seeds around the bulb and 8 thorns on stem—none under left leaf. R. 4.
8 *thorns.*

<h2 style="text-align:center">No. 307.</h2>

Obv. Same as No. 300.
Rev. Same as No. 306. R. 4.
8 *thorns.*

<h2 style="text-align:center">No. 308.</h2>

Obv. Resembles No. 297, but the lower part of coil ends inside of the middle part, instead of ending outside, as all others do; the lock is heavier, particularly so at its junction with the coil. In SCOTIA, the upper stroke of letter s is double-cut and the T is closer to I.
Rev. Same as No. 306. R. 3.
8 *thorns.*

1840. Pennies.

<h2 style="text-align:center">No. 309.</h2>

Obv. Similar. The lock from coil is large, there are 5 well defined fringes of hair on neck; the ear inclines to right.
Rev. ONE PENNY TOKEN, 1840. There are 15 seeds around the thistle bulb, and the fourth notch from bottom on the outside of right leaf is very deep. R. 4.

No. 310.

Obv. Closely resembles No. 309, but the lock from coil is shorter and heavier; there are only 4 fringes on the neck, but larger.
Rev. The thistle bulb has 16 seeds around, and the stem longer. R. 8.

No. 311.

Obv. Small lock from hair coil; 7 delicate fringes on the neck; the ear stands upright.
Rev. Same as No. 309.   R. 1.

1843.   Pennies.

No. 312.

Obv. Same as No. 310.
Rev. Similar, dated 1843.   There are 17 seeds around the bulb; the fourth notch from bottom on the outside of right leaf is very light.   R. 5.

No. 313.

Obv. Same as No. 310.
Rev. Same as No. 309, but a " 3 " has been sunk over the " 0 " in the date, making it read 1843.
This is what is generally known as an " over-date ".   R. 8.

No. 314.

Obv. Same as No. 311.
Rev. Same as No. 312.   R. 3.

SEMI-OFFICIAL ISSUE

No. 315.

Obv. Bust of Victoria to the left. VICTORIA D : G : BRITAN-
NIAR : REG : F : D : 1856.

Rev. May flowers. PROVINCE OF NOVA SCOTIA— HALFPENNY
TOKEN. Edge plain. Bronze and gilted. R. 1.

No. 316.

Same as No. 315, but Brass. R. 3.

No. 317.

Same as No. 315, but with the engraver's initials —L. C. W.—
under bust, and the figures in the date closer. R. 8.

This variety is illustrated in Messrs. Ralph Heaton, Sons &
Co.'s book, giving an illustration record of the coins they have struck.

No. 318.

Similar, but ONE PENNY TOKEN. R. 1.

No. 319.

Same as No. 318, but has the same initial letters under the
bust as No. 317. R. 1.

No. 320.

Obv. Bust of Victoria to the left. VICTORIA D : G : BRITT :
REG : F : D :

Rev. Crown and date " 1861 " within a small, ornamental
circle. A wreath composed of may flowers, roses, may flower and
rose leaves around border with HALF CENT above, and NOVA SCOTIA
below. R. 1.

No. 321.

Same as No. 320, date 1864. R. 1.

No. 322.

Obv. Similar. ONE CENT 1861. R. 1.

No. 323.

Same as No. 322. Date 1862. R. 3.

No. 324.

Same as No. 322. Date 1864. R. 1.

BROKE TOKENS

From an historical point of view this series, although small, should prove interesting to all Canadians and particularly so to Collectors. From the absence of any indication of value these might be looked upon as a medallet rather than a token, though doubtless they passed as currency with the others. As the fact also occurred to the Wellington wars tokens, a specimen of which resembles in workmanship No. 325.

They were undoubtedly issued by retail merchants of Nova Scotia. Some varieties are plentiful, while others are somewhat difficult to obtain, especially in fine condition. No. 329 is unique so far.

No. 325.

Obv. Bust of Commander Broke to the left. BROKE—HALIFAX NOVA SCOTIA. The coat has 3 buttons, one fastening the shoulder strap of the epaulet to the collar, and 2 on coat proper, between which there is a military ribbon. This is the longest bust of the series.

Rev. Britannia seated to the left. BRITANNIA 1814. The female holds an olive sprig in her right hand and a trident in her left, the right tine of which touches letter I. Edge milled. R. 3.

No. 326.

Obv. Bust smaller. The coat has 4 buttons, including the one fastening shoulder strap, which is high in relief, the lower one is large and on line of truncation. A break shows in the die extending across the letters OTI in SCOTIA.

Rev. The female figure has a braid of hair around the head; the trident is distant from letters; the mainmasts of both ships are of equal height. R. 5.

No. 327.

Obv. The coat has only 3 buttons, with none on shoulder strap. In SCOTIA, the letter s almost touches c.

Rev. There is no braid of hair around female head; the mainmast of right ship is higher than that of the left, the ground is farther from border. R. 2.

No. 328.

Obv. Same as No. 327.
Rev. Same as No. 326. R. 6.

No. 329.

Obv. Closely resembles No. 327, but the coat has 4 buttons, one on shoulder strap and 3 on coat proper; those on coat are smaller and the lower one is above line of truncation and closer to lapel. In legend, the letters are differently spaced, especially so in SCOTIA where the c is a trifle closer to o than to s. R. 9.

Rev. Same as No. 327.

———————

TOKENS AND MERCHANTS' CARDS

No. 330.

Obv. Ship. NOVA SCOTIA AND NEW BRUNSWICK. In exergue SUCCESS.

Rev. Female seated on a bale of goods, to the left, holding a pair of scales in her right hand and a cornucopia in her left, representing Commerce. HALFPENNY TOKEN. Oblique milling on edge. R. 6.

No. 331.

Obv. Bust to the right.   HALF PENNY TOKEN, 1814.   The right top-leaf points to second N in PENNY.

Rev. Ship.   PAYABLE BY CARRITT & ALPORT, in exergue HALIFAX. The bowsprit extends above O in ALPORT.   Borders of dots and edge engrailed.   R. 3.

No. 332.

This token closely resembles preceding one, but the two laurel leaves at the top are directly under first N, and the bowsprit of the ship on reverse points to the center of letter O.   Small serratures on borders and edge plain.   R. 9.

This variety is very rare, there being only two or three specimens known.   Mr. W. W. C. Wilson, of Montreal, is the owner of the one sold in the Stickney Collection.

No. 333.

Obv. Same as No. 331.

Rev. Ship.   FOR THE CONVENIENCE OF TRADE.   R. 5.

The ship shown on the three foregoing tokens doubtless represents the " Shannon."

No. 334.

Same as No. 333, but in brass.   R. 6.

No. 335.

Obv. Bust to right within a circle.   HALFPENNY TOKEN, 1814.

Rev. Building.   PAYABLE BY HOSTERMAN & ETTER— HALIFAX. R. 4.

No. 336.

Obv. Similar, but without circle around the bust.   Date 1815. The laurel wreath has 6 leaves, the date is large and widely spaced, the 5 nearly touches drapery.

Rev. The design is smaller and the letters are closer together. R. 2.

No. 337.

Same as No. 336, but some of the windows to the building are not sashed.   R. 3.

No. 338.

Obv. Indian and dog.   STAR & SHANNON HALIFAX, 1815.
Rev. Ship.   HALFPENNY TOKEN—NOVA SCOTIA.   Engrailed edge.
R. 2.

No. 339.

Same as No. 338, but edge plain and struck on thin flan.   R. 3.

No. 340.

Obv. Similar.   COMMERCIAL CHANGE, 1815.
Rev. Same as No. 338.   Edge engrailed.   R. 3.

No. 341.

Obv. Cask.   HALF PENNY TOKEN, 1815.
Rev. PAYABLE / BY / MILES W. / WHITE / HALIFAX / N.S. in six lines.
Around border IMPORTER OF IRONMONGERY HARDWARES &C.   Plain
edge.   R. 3.

No. 342.

Obv. Bust to the right.   HALF PENNY TOKEN, 1815.   Large head
laureated with 8 leaves; date small and compact, the figure 5 stands
very close to drapery.
Rev. Ship.   PAYABLE BY JOHN ALEX^R BARRY—HALIFAX.   R. 4.

No. 343.

Obv. Similar.   Slender bust with 7 leaves to the wreath; large
date widely spaced, the two last figures are close to drapery.
Rev. Same as No. 342.   R. 5.

<h2 align="center">No. 344.</h2>

Same as No. 343, but in brass.   R. 6.

<h2 align="center">No. 345.</h2>

Obv. Similar. Small bust with 7 leaves to the wreath; the date is large, compact and distant from drapery.
Rev. Same as No. 342.   R. 3.

<h2 align="center">No. 346.</h2>

Obv. Bust to the right.   GENUINE BRITISH COPPER, 1815.
Rev. Britannia seated to left.   HALF PENNY TOKEN.   Edge milled.   R. 5.

<h2 align="center">No. 347.</h2>

Obv. Same as No. 342.
Rev. Britannia seated to left.   GENUINE BRITISH COPPER.   The female holds an olive sprig of 9 leaves in her right hand, the upper leaf of which extends between the letters E and B.   The legend is distant from the ground.   Edge plain.   R. 3.

<h2 align="center">No. 348.</h2>

Obv. Same as No. 343.
Rev. Similar to No. 347, but the sprig in the female's right hand has only 4 leaves, and the ground is closer to legend.   R. 2.

<h2 align="center">No. 349.</h2>

Obv. Same as No. 336.
Rev. Same as No. 348.   R. 4.

<h2 align="center">No. 350.</h2>

Obv. Same as No. 345.
Rev. Same as No. 348.   R. 7.

26

No. 351.

Obv. Similar. There is no hair between laurel top-leaves, the truncation forms a convex line to the left.
Rev. Ship. beneath HALIFAX. Edge milled. R. 3.

No. 352.

Obv. A close copy of No. 351, but the hair extends above and beyond second leaf at top, and the truncation forms a concave line to left.
Rev. Same as No. 351. R. 4.

No. 353.

Obv. Similar. There are 8 leaves to the laurel wreath with 2 at top.
Rev. Ship. SUCCESS TO NAVIGATION & TRADE. The ship has a large flag at the stern, and the water ends in one wave to the right. Edge plain. R. 4.
8 *leaves and large flag variety.*

No. 354.

Obv. Same as No. 353.
Rev. Closely resembles the last, but the ship has a smaller flag and the water ends in 2 waves to the right. R. 3.
8 *leaves and small flag variety.*

No. 355.

Obv. Similar to No. 353, but smaller bust. There are 6 leaves to the wreath with only one at the top.
Rev. Same as No. 353. R. 6.
6 *leaves and large flag variety.*

No. 356.

Obv. Same as No. 355.
Rev. Same as No. 354. R. 2.
6 *leaves and small flag variety.*

No. 357.

Obv. Building. WHOLESALE & RETAIL HARDWARE STORE. Underneath building 1816.
Rev. Cask, spade and shovel, scythe and sickle. PAYABLE AT W. A. & S. BLACK'S HALIFAX.N. S. R. 4.

No. 358.

Obv. Same as No. 357.
Rev. Similar, but with HALIFAX above, and NOVA SCOTIA below. The firm's name being omitted. R. 4.

No. 359.

Obv. A thistle sprig. NEMO ME IMPUNE LACESSIT.
Rev. Ship. PAYABLE AT THE STORE OF J. BROWN. Edge milled. R. 2.

No. 360.

Obv. Building, above HALF PENNY.
Rev. J. B. in script. Edge plain. R. 6.

No. 361.

Obv. Same as No. 360.
Rev. A harp within a delicate wreath. R. 9.
This coin seems to me rare as there are only two specimens known so far, one in the collection of Mr. R. W. McLachlan and the other in my own. As it will be noted by the illustration of the reverse, the latter is in poor state of preservation.

The similarity of the building shown on these two pieces, Nos. 360 and 361, to that appearing on the Blacks' tokens has induced me to class them among this series. And further, it has been claimed that the initials J. B. on the reverse of one of them stand for John Brown, the issuer of No. 359.

<h2 style="text-align:center">No. 362.</h2>

Obv. In field, CHEAP / DRY GOODS / STORE in three curved lines, around the border W. L. WHITE'S—HALIFAX HOUSE HALIFAX.

Rev. In field, ONE / FARTHING in two lines, around border PAYABLE AT W. L. WHITE'S—HALIFAX HOUSE HALIFAX N. S.   R. 5.

<h2 style="text-align:center">No. 363.</h2>

Obv. Closely resembles No. 362, but in CHEAP DRY GOODS STORE, the letters are closer together, and the D in DRY is directly under C in CHEAP.

Rev. Same as No. 362.   R. 9.

I only know of one specimen to be in existence, and it is in the collection of Mr. Thomas Wilson, of Montreal.

<h2 style="text-align:center">No. 364.</h2>

Obv. Steamboat.   HALIFAX STEAMBOAT COMPANY.

Rev. FERRY / TOKEN in two lines.   R. 2.

<h2 style="text-align:center">No. 365.</h2>

Obv. ROBERT PURVES—CHEAP / FAMILY / STORE—WALLACE.

Rev. In field ENCOURAGE / COUNTRY / IMPORTERS in three lines. R. 2.

This token is evidently a much later issue.

OBVERSES

THE COINS AND TOKENS OF NOVA SCOTIA, BY EUGENE G. COURTEAU, M.D.

REVERSES

THE COINS AND TOKENS OF NOVA SCOTIA BY EUGENE G. COURTEAU, M.D.

OBVERSES

THE COINS AND TOKENS OF NOVA SCOTIA BY EUGENE G. COURTEAU, M.D.

REVERSES

The Coins and Tokens of Nova Scotia by Eugene G. Courteau, M.D.

PLATE V

OBVERSES

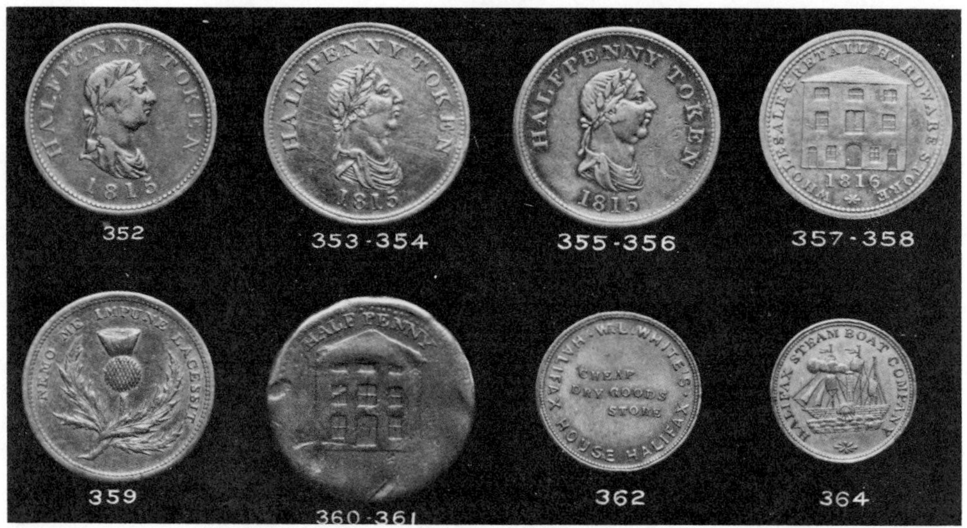

REVERSES

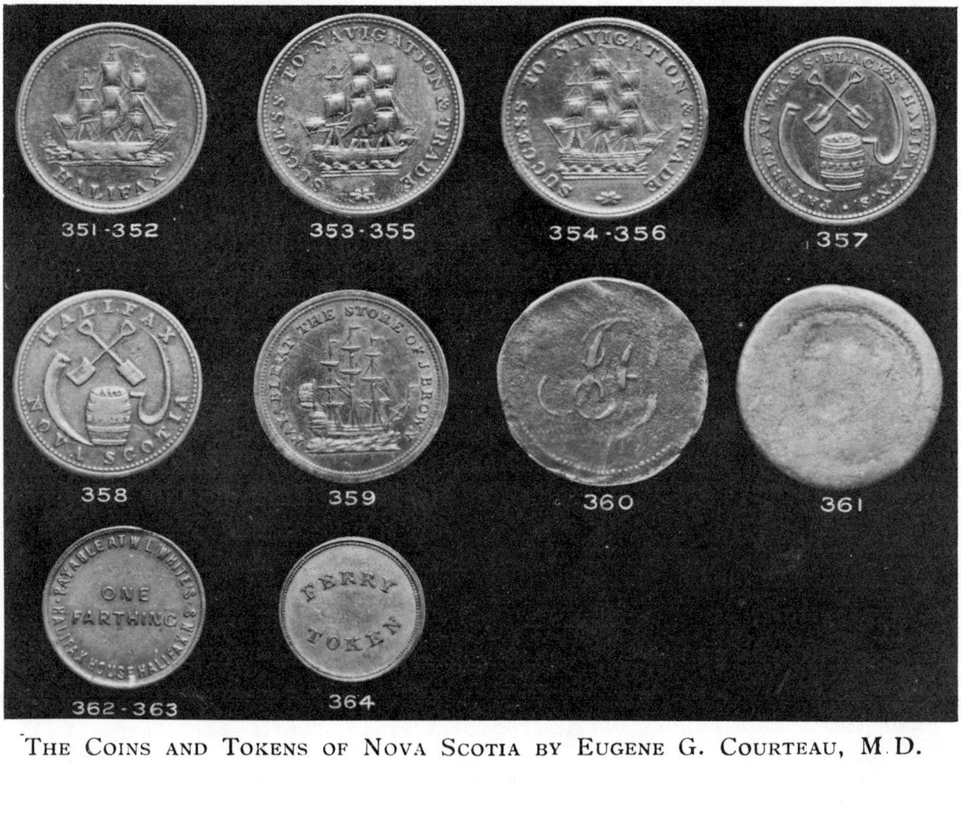

THE COINS AND TOKENS OF NOVA SCOTIA BY EUGENE G. COURTEAU, M.D.

OBVERSES

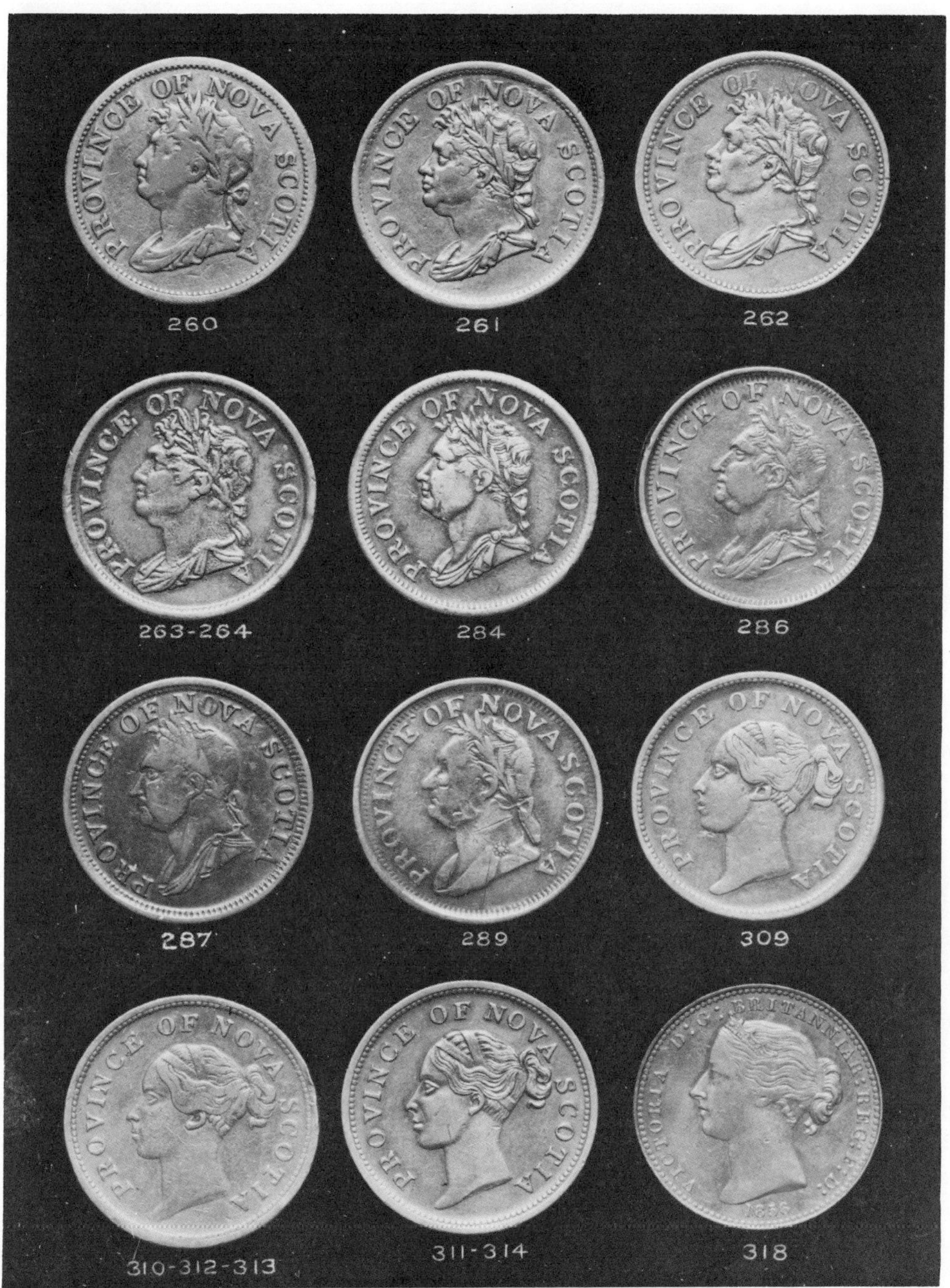

The Coins and Tokens of Nova Scotia by Eugene G. Courteau, M.D.

REVERSES

THE COINS AND TOKENS OF NOVA SCOTIA BY EUGENE G. COURTEAU, M.D.